T0378825

Career-Ready Kids

BUILD AND MOVE

Diane Lindsey Reeves

21st Century Junior Library

Published in the United States of America by:

CHERRY LAKE PRESS
2395 South Huron Parkway, Suite 200, Ann Arbor, Michigan 48104
www.cherrylakepress.com

Reading Adviser: Beth Walker Gambro, MS, Ed., Reading Consultant, Yorkville, IL

Photo Credits: © Red Fox studio/Shutterstock, cover; © Somchai_Stock/Shutterstock, 5; © Phonlamai
Photo/Shutterstock, 6; © Emre Ucarer/Shutterstock, 7; © Bricolage/Shutterstock, 8; © Robert Kneschke/
Shutterstock, 10–11; © alvarog1970/Shutterstock, 13; © Madeleine Deaton/Shutterstock, 14;
© Sach336699/Shutterstock, 16; © ME Image/Shutterstock, 19; © pikselstock/Shutterstock, 21

Cherry Lake Press is an imprint of Cherry Lake Publishing Group.

Library of Congress Cataloging-in-Publication Data has been filed and is available at catalog.loc.gov.

Cherry Lake Publishing Group would like to acknowledge the work of the Partnership for 21st Century Learning,
a Network of Battelle for Kids. Please visit Battelle for Kids online for more information.

Printed in the United States of America

Note from publisher: Websites change regularly, and their future contents are outside of our control.
Supervise children when conducting any recommended online searches for extended learning opportunities.

CONTENTS

DISCOVER THE BUILDING AND MOVING CAREER CLUSTER

Raise your hand if you like making things! This cluster from the National Career Clusters® Framework calls for builders and makers. It has careers that build homes. It has careers that build skyscrapers. It has careers that build bridges. It has careers that make everything from chewing gum to rocket ships. Moving careers are designed to get all these products where they need to go.

There are many different careers to choose from in the Building and Moving cluster. These workers are building a roof.

Some of these careers involve making things. Some involve building places. These are the places where people live. They are places where people work and play.

Some involve **advanced manufacturing**. This is manufacturing plus technology. Robots are coming to the rescue on assembly lines everywhere. But humans are still needed to help with production tasks.

Companies save time and money by using robots for assembly line tasks. Humans still help, but in different ways!

Look!

Look around to find a construction site in your community. Pay attention to the people and the processes they're using. Keep track of the trucks and heavy equipment, too.

People also design and operate the robots and systems that help make things faster.

Some of these careers involve moving things. Building and making things take lots of supplies. Raw materials come from all over the world. **Supply chain** careers move these supplies. They also move finished products. They move these things to places where they are made and sold.

Many trade workers teach to pass on the skills they've gained from experience.

You can take different training paths for Building and Moving careers. Some of the careers require college degrees. But many hands-on careers are learned in **trade schools**. They're learned through on-the-job training. **Apprenticeships** offer the chance to earn money while you learn.

Let's explore the three Building and Moving career areas:

- Construction
- Advanced Manufacturing
- Supply Chain and Transportation

Create!

Where did the food in your lunch come from? Moving careers transport your food! Create a map. With an adult, search online for the locations of different farms and factories. On your map, show each food's journey from farm and factory to your lunch!

EXPLORE BUILDING AND MOVING CAREERS

Many construction careers use both brain *and* muscle power. Some people do skilled trades. These are people like carpenters, electricians, and plumbers. They use their hands to get the job done. Other construction jobs use technology to do the heavy lifting. These include architects and drone operators.

No matter the trade, safety is key. Many building professionals wear hard hats.

Manufacturing jobs have changed a lot in recent years. Many are now advanced manufacturing jobs. People used to put products together piece by piece. Now robots and other machines make the process easier. Designing robots and managing **automated** processes are well-paid careers in this area.

Big world events can make products hard to get. Things like global pandemics or wars can affect the supply chain. This reminds us how important supply chain and transportation careers are.

Warehouse manager is an important supply chain career.

Have you always liked trains? Maybe you could drive one as a career!

239

Together, these jobs help move products from places where they are made to places where they are used. The U.S. transportation system moves a lot! It moves about 55.5 million tons of goods every day!

Would you like to help move products? Or does making or building things sound good to you? Either way, you'll want to explore career ideas in the Building and Moving career cluster.

Make a Guess!

Can you guess the most popular building material in history? Hint: You walk on it on your way to school. Answer: Concrete! Even the ancient Romans used it. They made it with lime, seawater, and volcanic ash.

Does working with your hands sound good to you? Then you're in the right career cluster.

IS BUILDING AND MOVING IN YOUR FUTURE?

Do you like putting things together? Are you interested in how things work? If your answer is yes, that's your first clue! Are you a big fan of planes, trains, and automobiles? Building and Moving careers might be a good choice for you.

There is no rush to decide. But it can be fun to check out the options. Figure out what you like to do.

Think of what you want to know more about. These clues will help narrow down your choices. Learn about yourself and explore different careers. These are good ways to be a career-ready kid.

You can experiment with career ideas, too. Ask an adult to help you talk to someone with a career that interests you. An adult can help you visit places where these people work. Think about what the work is like. Imagine the kinds of problems you can solve.

Being a career-ready kid **motivates** you to do your best work now. You can build a bridge from learning in school to preparing for your future career.

Think!

The assembly line was made popular by automaker Henry Ford. It changed the way cars and other products were made. See what you can learn about it to explain why it was such a brilliant idea.

Drone operators often work at construction sites. They use drones for inspections.

INVESTIGATING BUILDING AND MOVING CAREERS

Management
- logistics manager
- production manager
- project manager
- sourcing manager
- transportation director

Hands-On
- airframe & power plant (A&P) technician
- assembler
- auto mechanic
- machinist

BUILD AND MOVE

Skilled Trade
- carpenter
- electrician
- welder

Designing & Analyzing
- architect
- civil engineer
- robotics engineer
- software designer
- data analyst
- purchasing agent

Technology
- CAD drafter
- nanotechnologist

ACTIVITY

Practice building! Work with an adult to build a birdhouse.

- Find a building guide online. Make a list of materials you will need. Make a list of tools you will use. Will you follow the guide exactly? Will you do anything differently?

- After you answer these questions, you're ready to start! Once your project is done, write about the experience. How did it feel to build something? What parts did you like?

Ask Questions!

How is advanced manufacturing different from traditional manufacturing? Can you find an example of a new advanced manufacturing career?

GLOSSARY

advanced manufacturing (uhd-VANST man-yuh-FAK-chuhr-ing) use of technology and state-of-the-art processes to improve the quality and cost of making products

apprenticeships (uh-PREN-tuh-ships) on-the-job training with classroom instruction that prepares workers for highly skilled careers

automated (AW-tuh-may-tuhd) describing a process that is controlled by a machine rather than a person

motivates (MOH-tuh-vayts) provides a person with a reason for taking action

supply chain (suh-PLIE CHAYN) complex system that moves raw materials and finished products to the places and people who need them

trade schools (TRAYD SKOOLZ) programs that provide hands-on training and education in skilled trades

FIND OUT MORE

Books

Faber, Polly. *Special Delivery: A Book's Journey Around the World.* Somerville, MA: Candlewick, 2023.

Reeves, Diane Lindsey. *What Construction Managers Need to Know.* Ann Arbor, MI: Cherry Lake Publishing, 2024.

Rhatigan, Joe. *Get a Job at the Construction Site.* Ann Arbor, MI: Cherry Lake Publishing, 2017.

Websites

Explore these online resources with an adult.

Manufacturing Resource Center: What's So Cool About Manufacturing?

National Center for Construction Education and Research (NCCER): Build Your Future

INDEX

ABOUT THE AUTHOR

Diane Lindsey Reeves writes books to help students of all ages find bright futures. She lives in North Carolina with her husband and a big kooky dog named Honey. She has four of the best grandkids in the world.